AF270689

Caracals

Julie Murray

abdobooks.com

Published by Abdo Kids, a division of ABDO, P.O. Box 398166, Minneapolis, Minnesota 55439.
Copyright © 2023 by Abdo Consulting Group, Inc. International copyrights reserved in all countries.
No part of this book may be reproduced in any form without written permission from the publisher.
Abdo Kids Junior™ is a trademark and logo of Abdo Kids.

Printed in the United States of America, North Mankato, Minnesota.

102022

012023

THIS BOOK CONTAINS
RECYCLED MATERIALS

Photo Credits: Getty Images, Minden Pictures, Shutterstock

Production Contributors: Teddy Borth, Jennie Forsberg, Grace Hansen

Design Contributors: Candice Keimig, Pakou Moua

Library of Congress Control Number: 2022937177
Publisher's Cataloging-in-Publication Data

Names: Murray, Julie, author.

Title: Caracals / by Julie Murray

Description: Minneapolis, Minnesota : Abdo Kids, 2023 | Series: Interesting animals | Includes online resources and index.

Identifiers: ISBN 9781098264130 (lib. bdg.) | ISBN 9781098264697 (ebook) | ISBN 9781098264970 (Read-to-Me ebook)

Subjects: LCSH: African wildcat--Juvenile literature. | Cats--Juvenile literature. | Cats--Behavior--Juvenile literature. | Animals--Juvenile literature. | Zoology--Juvenile literature.

Classification: DDC 599.75--dc23

Table of Contents

Caracals

Caracals live in Africa and western Asia.

North America
Europe
Asia
Africa
South America
Australia
N
E
S
W

5

They live in forests and

grassy **plains**.

Caracals are medium-sized **wild** cats.

They have a strong body.

They can weigh more

than 40 pounds (18 kg).

Their fur is tan and white.
They have black markings
on their face.

Their ears are big and pointed with long, black **tufts**.

Caracals are fast! They can run up to 50 miles per hour (80 kph).

They are good climbers.

They can jump high too!

They jump to catch birds.
They also eat other small
animals.

Caracal Features

black markings on face

pointed ears with tufts

strong body

tan and white fur

Glossary

plain

a large, flat area of land with few or no trees, sometimes covered by long grass.

tuft

a group or clump of long strands of hair.

wild

living in a natural state; not tamed.

Index

Visit **abdokids.com** to access crafts, games, videos, and more!